Bitcoin Useful Tips
The Secret of Cryptocurrencies

Hermann Logang

and

Saradienne Gourgue

Copyright

No part or any portion of this book may be reproduced, distributed, or used in any manner whatsoever without the prior written permission of the publisher, except for the use of brief quotations in a critical review or certain other noncommercial uses permitted by copyright laws.

© 2018 Hermann Logang and Saradienne Gourgue
All rights reserved.

ISBN: 1984267256
ISBN 13: 9781984267252

Disclaimer

Information provided in this book is intended exclusively for informational purposes only. The high volatility of cryptocurrencies significantly affects their value, which is characterized by significant up and downtrends. We recommend that novices and even experienced investors always seek professional advice before making any crypto-investment decision.

Contents

Disclaimer

Preface — 5

Acknowledgments — 6

Introduction — 7

Chapter 1   Cryptocurrency: Bitcoin and Its Genesis — 8

Chapter 2   Obtaining and Securing Bitcoins and Altcoins — 12

Chapter 3   Online Exchanges — 19

Chapter 4   Investment Strategies — 23

Chapter 5   How to Build Your Cryptocurrency Portfolio — 28

Chapter 6   Useful Rules of Cryptocurrency Trading — 36

Chapter 7   Trading Tips — 39

Chapter 8   Common Cryptocurrency Hacks and Scams — 43

Chapter 9   How to Minimize the Hacking of Your Coins — 48

Chapter 10   Understanding the Risks — 52

Chapter 11   Legality of Cryptocurrency — 56

Preface

The high *volatility*[1] of bitcoin and other altcoins labels them as extremely risky investments. Cryptocurrencies continue to attract investors because of their potential to yield greater returns. As more stakeholders invest in this pecuniary asset, understanding the risk associated with this type of investment is paramount. While we provide readers, pundits, investors, and other inquisitive minds with tools, tips, and strategies for understanding and reaching sound investment decisions, it is ultimately their decision to venture into the complex world of digital currencies.

However, it is important to understand that in the United States cryptocurrencies are not classified as currency, like the US dollar, but rather as a property or commodity. Furthermore, the government and the central bank do not back these digital assets. Therefore, your decision to invest carries a significant risk.

Acknowledgments

The completion of this book could not have been possible without the support of many valued and talented individuals whose names have not been mentioned herein. Their contributions are truly acknowledged and gratefully appreciated. The great minds behind this book dreamed and ventured into the crypto world to understand and share their knowledge with posterity. To all relatives, friends, and others who supported us, we sincerely thank you.

Introduction

Who could have thought that a *digital asset*[2] such as *bitcoin*[3] would attract such tremendous attention? In recent years, bitcoin, in particular, and *cryptocurrency*,[4] in general, have generated a lot of curiosity and have spawned an extraordinary amount of investment capital. As the frenzy and investment interest in cryptocurrency increase, it is important to offer readers the tools necessary for understanding and investing in this class of asset.

Opportunities abound in the highly speculative market of *digital currency*.[5] What are some strategies for a successful investment? What are the challenges facing bitcoin and other *altcoins*?[6] What should investors know to protect their investment?

This book addresses these questions and helps you familiarize yourself with cryptocurrencies. It provides guidance to current and potential investors and analyzes challenges facing this class of assets.

Chapter 1

Cryptocurrency: Bitcoin and Its Genesis

What Is a Cryptocurrency?

A cryptocurrency is a virtual asset or, more specifically, a digital currency that uses *cryptography*[7] to secure its transactions, generate new pecuniary units and secure existing ones, and verify its transfer. Its *decentralized*[8] nature has freed it from any governmental oversight, consequentially making it difficult to manipulate. The first cryptocurrency ever created was the bitcoin. To date, there is a plethora of cryptocurrencies in existence worldwide, each built on a specific project or platform. Examples include bitcoin, litecoin, ethereum, ripple, and monero.

What Is Bitcoin?

Bitcoin is a decentralized virtual currency used worldwide for transactions. It is exchangeable for services, products, and other digital currencies. No single financial or governmental institution controls bitcoin's network. However, government regulations affect its value and the value of all other cryptocurrencies. Cryptocurrency transactions are verified and *confirmed*[9] using a network of data communication supported by a *peer-to-peer network*.[10] All transactions are recorded in a decentralized public ledger called *blockchain*.[11]

Genesis of Bitcoin

A software developer named *Satoshi*[12] Nakamoto is credited with initiating the concept of blockchain and solving the *double spend*[13] enigma of digital currencies. However, his exact identity remains unclear. His initial concept of creating bitcoin was to craft a currency independent of any government or financial institution. This virtual currency had to be transferable electronically more or less instantly and with very low transaction fees. Nakamoto registered the domain name bitcoin.org and developed the bitcoin software as an *open-source code*.[14] Using his software, he mined the first fifty bitcoins, therefore officially launching bitcoin. Since then, bitcoin has undergone significant growth with many ups and downs and has become a center of attention for many investors.

Some Features of Bitcoin

Bitcoin includes the following features. It

- can not be counterfeited or reversed arbitrarily by the sender;

- eliminates third parties in its transaction;
- is accessible to everyone;
- provides controlled, fast, and secure global transactions;
- can be sent anywhere and delivered as soon as the bitcoin network processes the transaction; and
- provides relative anonymity by rendering it nearly impossible to track a particular bitcoin address to a person.

Is Bitcoin a Currency or a Commodity?

Bitcoin was designed to be a digital currency. It is accepted as such in some countries, whereas other countries have either banned it or branded it a commodity or property. In the United States, the Internal Revenue Service (IRS) classifies it as property. However, an increasing number of US companies are accepting bitcoin as a method of payment.

Currently bitcoin does not meet all the prerequisite characteristics required to be classified as true currency, such as durability, portability, divisibility, uniformity, limited supply, and acceptability. Moreover, it can not store value because of its high volatility.

The relative stability of a payment instrument is essential for pricing in an exchange or a market.

Bitcoin's constant wide fluctuation makes it less appropriate to be used as pricing tool for markets. It is difficult to envision bitcoin as a reliable potential currency, because it does not have a stable value. Instead, it fits more or less the classification of a commodity because of its substantial *fungibility*[15] and because its value is easily affected by market expectations.

Chapter 2

Obtaining and Securing Bitcoins and Altcoins

How to Get Bitcoins

There are many possibilities available for procuring bitcoins. The mainstream method is to purchase them from various online exchanges. They can be purchased using cash, credit- and debit-card transfers, bank transfers or wires, or even other cryptocurrencies. They are also transferrable from one individual to another one. Bitcoins can also be obtained by the process of *mining*.[16] Mining is the process that validates transactions and adds those transactions to the public ledger. Miners are rewarded with new bitcoins once they have successfully executed and deciphered complex puzzles, hence confirming executed transactions. Just like bitcoin, other cryptocurrencies can be purchased, mined, obtained in exchange of goods or services, or transferred as a gift or donation.

Criteria to Use When Buying Bitcoins or Altcoins Online

Before buying bitcoins from any online website, it is important to check for the following information about that exchange:

- **Reputation:** The most reliable method for inquiring about an exchange's reputation is reviewing its ratings from online sources or previous buyers. Activities that compromise the reputation of an exchange include negative opinions, association with illegal activities, lack of security leading to hackings, and frequent shutdowns, to name a few.

- **Fees:** Fees vary significantly from one exchange to another. Before you join any cryptocurrency marketplace, it is important to understand all related transaction fees. Transaction fees vary according to the time of the day. These fees are expressed in Satoshi (0.00000001 BTC^{17}) per byte of transaction data. Miners generally prioritize transactions with the highest fee per byte.

- **Payment options offered by the exchange:** Some of the available payment modalities include credit- and debit-card payments, wire transfers, bank drafts, cash, and PayPal. Exchanges that offer limited payment options may not be convenient. Purchasing cryptocurrencies with a credit card comes with a premium price and higher transaction and processing fees. Using a debit or credit card takes significantly less time than a bank draft or wire transfer.

- **Verification requirements:** Most trading platforms require identification verification in order to make deposits and withdrawals. The verification process is aimed at protecting the exchange against scams and money laundering. As the government continues to crack down on illegal activities in the crypto world, exchanges are required to properly identify all investors registered on their platform.

- **Geographical restrictions:** Some specific user functions offered by exchanges are only accessible from certain countries. Only join exchanges that allow full access to all platform tools and functions in your country of residence.

- **Exchange rate:** It is important to inquire about the cost of trading. It's not uncommon for rates to fluctuate up to 10 percent and even higher in some instances.

How to Store Bitcoins and Other Cryptocurrencies

Bitcoin and altcoins are stored in wallets. Not all cryptocurrencies can be stored in a wallet. Newer wallets now include the capability of storing a wide range of cryptocurrencies. A wallet is a collection of *private keys*[18] run by a program or software. The program manages the *coin's*[19] private key and also allows individuals to make transactions on the crypto network. A cryptocurrency wallet is similar to a traditional wallet, except that it is used to store a collection of bitcoin private keys rather than dollar bills and debit and credit cards. Crypto wallets are categorized as either cold or hot. Hot wallets are connected to the Internet, whereas cold wallets are offline or disconnected from the Internet.

Hot Wallet

Hot wallets, also called web-based wallets, are apps or programs run on any computer or phone with Internet connectivity. They are called hot wallets because they are connected to the Internet. Examples of hot wallets include mobile wallets, desktop wallets, and online wallets:

- **Mobile wallets:** Apps run on a smartphone. These apps store bitcoin private-key addresses and enable transactions to be done directly with a phone. Examples of mobile wallets include the Android-based bitcoin wallet, mycelium, xapo, and blockchain.

- **Desktop wallets:** Computer programs that store bitcoin's private key on a hard drive. This wallet is hosted on a desktop and is not portable on an individual. Some pundits consider it a cold wallet, because of its ability to store your private key on a hard drive. With this type of wallet, your private-key exposure to online hacking is reduced because your key is saved on a hard drive. Nonetheless, your wallet could still be exposed to cyber attacks if your desktop is infected with malware. Desktop wallets are more secure than mobile wallets because they are more difficult to steal.

- **Online wallets:** Websites that allow bitcoin to be stored on a server. These websites hold your private keys. There have been numerous reported cases of compromised online web wallets. Examples of online wallets include blockchain.info, Coinbase, and so on. Online web wallets are appropriate for storing small amounts and making minor transactions. It is not safe to hold a large amount of bitcoins in such wallets. The main advantage of online wallets is their easy accessibility and lower cost of executing transactions; however, they carry a higher risk of being compromised.

Cold Wallets

Cold wallets are offline wallets and refer to the use of devices not connected to the Internet to keep bitcoin and altcoins. Cold wallets include hardware wallets, paper wallets, and physical coins:

- **Hardware wallets:** Dedicated devices use to keep private keys electronically and facilitate payments. Hardware wallets are similar to USB keys, which can be carried around. They are resilient to attacks by any malware. Examples include Trezor, Ledger, Nano S, and KeepKey.

- **Paper wallets:** Very secure way of storing bitcoins, because they are not exposed to malware. However, if lost, they will not be recovered, because there is no software support for such wallets. They can easily be securely stored in safes and safe deposit boxes.

- **Physical bitcoins:** Bearer instrument that represents bitcoin itself. The physical coin comes with a tamper-proof sticker. The coin is purchased at a small premium above its actual value to cover the cost of manufacturing and shipping.

Best Way to Store Bitcoin and Other Altcoins

Cold storage offers the safest method for storing coins because of its greatest safety profile. This method of storage disconnects your coins from the Internet, rendering them inaccessible to the preying interests of malware and hackers. Cold storage's high-end *encryption*[20] feature deters the toughest cyber attacks. However, regardless of the method of storage used, it is very important to never disclose your private key to anyone.

Chapter 3

Online Exchanges

There are many online bitcoin exchanges, and new ones are frequently created. Regardless of the exchange chosen, there are transactions fees associated with buying or selling coins. These fees depend on the payment method, the dollar value of the transaction, and the exchange where the transaction is executed. Here are descriptions of a few of them.

Coinbase

A US-based platform operating from San Francisco, Coinbase provides the easiest and most popular way to buy some cryptocurrencies online. The first step is to sign up for a Coinbase account at coinbase.com. A verification e-mail is sent to the e-mail address you provide. Like all major exchanges, Coinbase requires a verification process that includes an ID submission. For safety purposes, set up a *two-factor authentication*,[21] thereby allowing Coinbase to request a special code from your mobile device when signing in or processing transactions. Coinbase provides Federal Deposit Insurance Corporation (FDIC) coverage for only cash balances and not cryptocurrencies.

Gemini

This US-based exchange has a similar account setup to Coinbase. This exchange platform is gaining popularity in many states. It provides FDIC insurance for cash balances only. No insurance is provided once you convert your cash into any form of cryptocurrency.

Kraken

This US-based exchange operates out of San Francisco. In order to register on this forum, create an account by entering your e-mail address, user ID, and password. After signing up, it is required to activate the account. Check the e-mail provided for an activation code. Before you are able to trade, you will have to first verify your account.

Bitstamp

This is an EU-based bitcoin marketplace that allows people from all over the world to safely buy and sell cryptocurrencies online. The first step is to sign up at https://www.bitstamp.net. Once you have registered, an e-mail containing a user ID and password is sent to you. You will have to provide a form of identification in order to verify the account. For safety purposes, set up two-factor authentication.

Cex.io

This exchange provides a wide range of trading possibilities for cryptocurrency users. The platform offers personalized and user-friendly trading dashboards and margin trading. CEX also offers a brokerage service that provides novice traders an extremely simple way to buy bitcoin at prices that are more or less in line with the market rate.

BitQuick

This platform is a US-based exchange that allows you to execute your purchase using cash deposit. Investors have the option to browse multiple offers and select the one they want. Upon picking the desired offer, the investor is required to make a cash deposit into the seller's account. The purchaser's account will then be credited with the purchased digital asset.

Some Cryptocurrency Exchanges

- Bisq — https://bisq.network
- Bitfinex — https://www.bitfinex.com
- Bitstamp — https://www.bitstamp.net
- BitQuick — https://bitquick.co
- Bittrex — https://bittrex.com
- CEX.IO — https://cex.io
- CoinATMradar — https://Coinatmradar.com
- Coinbase — https://www.coinbase.com
- CoinMama — https://www.coinmama.com
- Gemini — https://Gemini.com
- GDAX — https://www.gdax.com
- Cryptopay — https://Cryptopay.me
- Kraken — https://www.kraken.com
- LocalBitcoins — https://localbitcoins.com
- Paxful — http://Paxful.com
- Poloniex — http://poloniex.com
- ShapeShift — https://shapeshift.io
- xCoins.io — https://Xcoins.io

Chapter 4

Investment Strategies

As cryptocurrencies draw the interest of various investors, a key question that always arises is, how should one invest? Just like for any speculative asset, there is not a right answer that suits every investor. We provide here a few investment ideas.

Buy and Hold

This consists of buying and holding coins with the hope that their value will increase on the long run. It is always recommended to buy well-known cryptocurrencies such as bitcoin, ethereum, dash, litecoin, or ripple. The use of this strategy does not require a timing of the market. Investors are advised to buy at any time, regardless of the price. Small price fluctuations do not significantly alter this strategy. One key advantage of this strategy is that it significantly reduces transaction costs. It is perfect for investors and traders looking to make potentially large gains with minimal time expenditure. A buy and hold strategy has a tax advantage if the hold is over a year because long-term investments are taxed at a lower rate than short-term investments.

Some Buy and Hold Tips

- Use larger time frames for technical analysis, such as daily, weekly, and monthly charts.
- If you are using stop losses, do not place them too close to your entry price.
- It is best to minimized leverage or not use it at all. Holding leveraged cryptocurrency trades for months or years can be costly.
- If possible, take advantage of pullbacks to get a better entry price.
- If the uptrend is nonvolatile and very strong, do not wait for deep *retracements.*[22] At-market entries may be considered in this instance, as well as breakout entries.

Microprofit Strategy

The goal of this strategy is to create small profits that add up over time. It allows investors to slowly grow their initial investment in very small incremental steps on an hourly, daily, weekly, or monthly basis. It is recommended to place your sell limit at 0.5 or 1 percent of the initial buy price. Remember to include trading fees in your calculation. These small incremental growths compound to bigger profit over time. Patience is key with this approach. This approach works best for day traders.

The Bollinger Bands Strategy

What Are Bollinger Bands?

Bollinger bands, developed by John Bollinger, are volatility measurement computed using standard deviation calculations. They consist of two bands placed above and below a moving average. The bands move far apart when volatility increases, and they narrow with a decrease in volatility. The bands are graphed on a cryptocurrency price chart. The chart illustrates prices of a coin over time and these prices are represented in the form of *candlesticks*.[23] Bollinger bands help understand the trend of the cryptocurrency. It also provides information about the volatility of the coin. Occasionally, Bollinger bands coil closely indicating that the stock is trading in a narrow range.

Setting Up Bollinger Bands

On your coin's chart, set up your graph to five, fifteen, or thirty-minute candlesticks. Also set the view of your graph for the last six, twelve, or twenty-four hours depending on the frequency at which you want to trade. Set your technical analysis on Bollinger bands.

The Bollinger band is the secret weapon that hints when to take a trade or not.

When to Take a Trade Based on Bollinger Bands

On your chart, identify areas called *Bollinger squeezes*.[24] These are areas where the two Bollinger bands come very close. Bollinger bands getting closer indicate that a trend is about to happen. Because Bollinger squeezes do not provide directional clues, another technical analysis can be used to anticipate or confirm the directional break. Do not trade when Bollinger bands are downtrending and the candles are below the two Bollinger bands. That generally means the trend will continue to be downward. Note that if there is a strong uptrend of the Bollinger bands during a Bollinger squeeze and the candles are up-trending too, it could mean that the price of the coin could continue to rise. It is important to remember that there is no certainty with cryptocurrency. Before trading any coin, always research its most current news.

How to Identify a Bollinger Directional Break

Look for volume-based indicators, such as the accumulation-distribution line, the money-flow index, or the on-balance volume. These indicators provide clues about the price direction. Signs of accumulation increase the chances of an upside breakout, while signs of distribution increase the chances of a downside break. In order to look for indicators signaling that the price could increase quickly, pay attention to all of the following: Bollinger squeeze, upward trend of the Bollinger band, and candles breaking out of the upper band.

Market-Correction Strategy

A market correction occurs when price declines temporarily during an uptrend. It could be of shorter duration compared to a bear market or a recession, but it can also be a precursor to the latter. It is important not to panic during a market correction and sell your investments. Generally, market corrections bounce back. The time it takes the market to crash is generally about the same or even longer as the time required for it to correct itself. This strategy requires patience. A consistent uptrend form a bearish market generally signal a reversal of trend. It is not unusual to see professional traders sell on a price downtrend and rebuy when the price of the coin is even lower. However, be aware that the price could reverse its trend, and you could rebuy at a higher price.

Chapter 5

How to Build Your Cryptocurrency Portfolio

Do Your Homework

It is unrealistic to invest in an asset without understanding it. Before investing in a cryptocurrency, research that cryptocurrency and its competitors. There are thousands of altcoins in existence. You are not required to know all of them, but you should at least have a good grasp of the major ones, such as bitcoin, ethereum, dash, litecoin, and ripple. Visit the following websites to acquaint yourself with cryptocurrencies: coinmarketcap.com, tradingview.com, and cryptomaps.org.

You should also understand the concept of cryptocurrencies and blockchain. Each cryptocurrency has a project or goal aimed at solving a problem; however, it is not unusual to find multiple cryptocurrencies with the same goal. It could be appealing to look at a currency and believe that it may be the solution that revolutionizes the marketplace. Nevertheless, it might actually be the worst solution available. Consider the following points when researching a coin.

1. *White Paper*[25]
    - Does the white paper encompass all the information and answers to your questions?
    - Does it make reference to scholarly articles to support its existence?
    - Can it be modified and amended to meet building platform requirements?
    - A white paper that is open to improvement is a clear indication that the developer is willing to make necessary changes to improve the coin and its technology.
    - Always read and understand the white paper.

2. *Vision and Market Validation*
    - What is the cryptocurrency's project, and does it solve a genuine societal concern or problem?
    - Is the platform a new concept, or does it improve an existing solution?
    - The easiest way to answer those questions is to read the cryptocurrency founder's white paper.

3. *Product Strength*
    - Is there an actual product, and is it working as described in the white paper?

- If the product is on the market, try out the software. If possible, and assess how it works or inquire from other users how it works.
- If the application or the product is at its early stage, could it be completed and implemented in a timely manner?
- What are the updates on the product? This can be very challenging. It is important to inquire about the product's status update and compare it to the goals and milestones set in the white paper.

4. Developer Strength and Experience
    - Is the team of developers experienced?
    - What is the ability of the development team to execute the goal or vision of the project?
    - Does the team have the required knowledge and skills to address the project's goal?
    - These questions are often difficult to answer. A good step for addressing any concerns is to read about the background of the founders and the information technology team. That information could be obtained in the white paper and even online. You can review their résumés to

assess if the team has the skill set to carry on the project.

5. Website
    - Go through the website and find out if it looks professional.
    - Does the website provide relevant information (vision, concept, and team)?
    - Does what is written make any sense?
    - Evaluating the presentation and content of the website is a personal judgment call, and opinions may vary from one investor to another one.

6. Market Value
    - What is the *valuation*[26] of the coin you are investing in?
    - Can the coin perform better in comparison to other cryptocurrencies?
    - A better way to think of this is to predict whether the application or platform will be adopted and used on a broader scale.
    - Inquire if there are potential breaches.
    - Is the product in the line with regulatory agencies?

Open a Cryptocurrency Account

Research the marketplace in order to choose what exchange to use to purchase your cryptocurrencies. When deciding your preferred cryptocurrency exchange, it is important to research it thoughtfully and read user reviews. Choose preferably exchanges that accept *fiat money*[27] deposit and allow you to buy your desired coin. Some exchanges provide limited options for purchasing coins. Examples of such exchanges include Coinbase, Gemini, and Fxchoice. Build your cryptocurrency portfolio by picking the coins you want to invest in. Make sure that your favorite cryptocurrency is traded on the exchange. Not all altcoins are listed on crypto exchanges.

Select Your Coins

Questions abound as to how to pick the right cryptocurrency. The answer many investors do not want to hear is that it is difficult to spot the perfect coin that will skyrocket in price overnight. However, doing your homework by researching the coin's feature will always lead you in the right direction. Regardless of whether you choose to invest in the long or short run, base your choice on the following recommendations.

Twenty-Four-Hour Volume

This indicates how much value of the coin has traded over a twenty-four-hour period. A rule of thumb is to pick coins with at least $10,000 trading volume. The higher the twenty-four-hour volume, the more established a coin is. It indicates that readers have trust in that specific coin.

However, be careful of pump-and-dump schemes, where developers buy the cryptocurrency in a large amount to drive the price up. Once the price peaks, they sell it immediately, leading to a consequential significant drop in the price. To avoid such schemes, look at the trading history and price graphs to identify steep curves. Pump-and-dump schemes do not generally last longer than a few days.

Coin Liquidity

It is measured by either the volume percentage or the bitcoin volume. To avoid coin liquidity scams, do not buy a coin with very small bitcoin volume, because a small purchase of few hundred could move the market to your disadvantage. Also trade only in credible exchanges with larger circulating coin volumes.

One scheme to watch for is wash trading, which occurs when an exchange artificially inflates the trading volume to attract traders. To circumvent it, pay attention to any increase in a coin volume that does not correspond to an increase in price.

Market Capitalization

This is the product of the current market price of a coin multiplied by the number of coins available. Developers have the tendency to issue more coins in order to inflate the perceived value of the coin. Coins with higher market capitalization attract more investors. A point of caution to consider is that market capitalization could also be inflated for coins that are newly introduced to the market. A low daily volume but high market capitalization for any coin is an indication of price manipulation.

Current Price

The current price of a coin is only an indicator of its perceived value. The price of the coin should certainly not be the determining criteria for purchasing it. Do not buy cryptocurrencies only because they are cheap.

Developer Activity

The credibility of the team behind the coin's platform is important. Pay attention to the following:

- **Updates about the coin:** New features could be added on a regular basis.
- **Original idea:** Many new altcoins could be simply a minor improvement of an already existing coin.
- **Developer responsiveness:** Prompt responses to investors' questions or concerns are preferable.
- **Core wallet for keeping the coin:** Many new altcoins do not have a major wallet to store them. That forces investors to keep them on the exchange, which is not a good idea.

Portfolio Makeup

It is recommended to build a portfolio with multiple cryptocurrencies. Always start with one coin and gradually diversify. There are wide varieties of cryptocurrencies worldwide that are available for trading. Pick a portfolio of coins with mid and large market capitalization.

Once you have selected your coins, visit other exchanges to compare their prices, market capitalizations, and trading volumes.

Chapter 6

Useful Rules of Cryptocurrency Trading

Avoid Greediness

Incremental microprofits add up to a larger profit. More often, people are tempted to wait until profits are enormous before they exit the market. However, slow and steady gains over time will generate more profit than trying to go too big. We recommend aiming for frequent 0.5 percent to 1 percent profits on trades.

It may seem small; however, consider making three to four successive trades per day with that small yield. At a 1.5 percent daily profit, a $1,000 investment will grow to close to $1,500 in a month and close to $3,800 in three months. This is assuming that all profits are reinvested. The advantage of the microprofit strategy is that if you pick the appropriate altcoins, you will always make these microprofits, regardless of market trends.

Trade in a Stable Coin

We suggest trading in either bitcoin or US dollar tethered (USDT). Trading in USDT provides a stable reference currency because the price of USDT does not change unlike other cryptocurrencies, which are always fluctuating. In addition, USDT is tied in value to the US dollar.

Bitcoin is relatively stable in comparison to other coins and has been increasing in value since its creation. Be aware that trading other coin using bitcoin as the reference currency subjects your investment to fluctuations of bitcoin, in addition to those of your coins. Never panic and sell when bitcoin is losing its value or when there is a market correction. There are strategies you can apply to even make money during a crash. Trading in bitcoin can magnify your profits if the price of bitcoin and your altcoin are both uptrending.

Only Trade after Identifying the Right Coin

Never be desperate for a trade. Only trade when there is an opportunity for growth. Never feel you have lost out or missed something because you did not take a trade. There are many opportunities to enter a trade every day, even in a bearish market.

Understand Fees and Taxes Associated with Trades

Whether you buy or sell a coin, there are taxes and fees associated with any trade. Trade on exchanges that provide minimal trade fees. Despite the fact that these fees are sometimes insignificant, they can add up to a larger amount, especially for those who execute multiple trades a day.

Accept Price Fluctuation

Cryptocurrencies are very volatile. A massive dip in price should not spell permanent disaster. Stay committed when you start heading into the red. Some observers believe that cryptocurrencies and particularly bitcoin are speculative bubbles. This argument has some merit and calls for caution when investing in cryptocurrency. However, it important to notice that the dot-com went through a bubble before becoming the foundation of today's Internet. Cryptocurrencies that survive over time will definitely be the technological innovation.

Chapter 7

Trading Tips

Tip One: Buy Low and Sell High

It is clearly difficult to identify ups and downs of the market because of altcoins' high volatility. Cryptocurrencies' value is very speculative and is subject to short-term variations. The reality is that it is very difficult to time a trade. A good recommendation is not to trade based on *hype*.[28] It is very challenging to identify peaks and valleys. Some exchanges allow placing limit orders to buy or sell at a precise price.

Tip Two: Trade Confidently

You should be confident prior to making any trade decision. There is no universal portfolio allocation that is right for everyone. The choice of a portfolio is contingent to your bankroll, risk tolerance, and time availability, to name a few. Day traders generally *buy the rumor and sell the news*.[29] If there is suspicion that the value is inflated due to hype, it is better to sell your coin early enough rather than too late. Even if you believe there is a possibility for more profits, the upside is sometimes not worth the risk.

Tip Three: Know Your Cryptocurrency

It is important to be informed about coin types and their relationship to market volatility. Certain coins tend to move with the market or with other coins, while others are negatively correlated. Do not allow emotions to influence your decisions.

Tip Four: Pay Attention to Market Capitalization

The market capitalization of a coin is more important than its price. The market capitalization of a coin is the price of that coin multiplied by the number of coins in circulation. The price of a coin is relevant only after accounting for the circulating supply. When purchasing coins, a key determinant is to focus on the percentage of that total market capitalization rather than the price of the coin.

Tip Five: Familiarize Yourself with Cryptocurrencies

There is a lot of information in print or online about the cryptocurrency ecosystem. Many websites have plenty of useful resources on coins and blockchains. Moreover, the investment world provides enough information to describe cryptocurrencies and offers guidance to invest in digital assets. Bitcoin and many other altcoins are available to traditional investors on many trading platforms.

Tip Six: Be Aware of the High Volatility

Never invest what you cannot afford to lose. Remember that gambling is a risk, and so is investing in cryptocurrency. The world of cryptocurrency is complicated and perplexing. It is better to have a good understanding of virtual currencies. First learn about cryptocurrencies and understand how bitcoin and blockchain function. Do not just look at the potential of larger earnings but also at the risk of losing everything.

Tip Seven: Invest Cautiously

Investing in cryptocurrencies carries a great risk due to their extreme volatility. Therefore, do not put all your eggs in the same basket. Many investors could be tempted to massively invest in cryptocurrencies after hearing their success stories. Remember that you will not be a millionaire overnight. Do not chase bitcoin prices. Timing is not a very important parameter in the cryptocurrency world.

Tip Eight: Choose a Strategy

Many strategies can be used when investing in cryptocurrencies. Those with the most success are often the most cautious ones. It is advisable to invest the same amount of money at the same frequency because it helps ride out the highs and the lows.

Tip Nine: Diversify Effectively

Diversification is a good approach, but it requires thought and effort. The best strategy is to hold on to your investment irrespective of the market volatility. Aside from bitcoin, there are many more altcoins that can be part of an investment portfolio. Focus on the top one hundred altcoins and carry a portfolio of a dozen coins. Many altcoins sometime perform well when bitcoin drops. Do not invest all your money into bitcoin.

Tip Ten: Keep Coins off the Exchanges

Hacking is rampant in the world of cryptocurrency. Keep your digital currencies offline in a safe cold wallet. Only maintain small number of coins in an online exchange. Understand that exchanges are not well regulated and that there are minimal government regulations and laws overseeing their activity.

Chapter 8

Common Cryptocurrency Hacks and Scams

An unsettling principle of online exchanges is that there is no absolute security. It is always possible over time to bypass security features. Hackers had with time, breached technologies that were previously considered secured. Anyone who invests in cryptocurrency is exposed to many risks, one of the most known being scamming. Some of the methods used by scammers can be remedied. It is however recommended that investors encrypt their Internet connection with a *virtual private network* [30] and use a dedicated computer to perform crypto transactions in order to safeguard their investment.

Hacked Exchanges

The popularity of cryptocurrencies has led to a rise in exchanges, some of which are untrustworthy. One strategy used by hackers is to access a legitimate exchange's server and create a spoof website filled with malware that remotely empties digital currency accounts. Hacking into exchanges is not uncommon and has been reported by many US cryptocurrency trading websites and Youbit, a South Korean digital currency exchange.

Phone Porting

Phone porting, also referred to as cell-phone identity theft, occurs when scammers seize an individual's phone number by misleading the mobile provider to allow access to the cell-phone account. Once they access the phone, they reset the password to the cryptocurrency account or wallet and drain the account. To avoid phone porting, it is recommended to include a unique PIN and verification question to your account to improve security. It is also a good practice to add two-factor authentication to all your crypto accounts in order to minimize phone porting.

Crypto-Stealing Malware

Scammers have developed a new type of cryptocurrency malware. The malware self-installs on your computer and tracks your login credentials or interferes with your transactions once you are logged in. Protecting your computer requires the use of a good antivirus software and a robust firewall system. Also use a two-factor authentication and a password manager to protect your login.

Fake Digital Wallets

Cryptocurrency users should be extremely careful when downloading wallets and surfing the web. There are numerous methods scammers use to steal cryptocurrency that include spoofing. There have been numerous reports of spoofing using fake mobile-apps wallets in the iTunes app store. These fake wallets operate by using names similar to existing official mobile-wallet apps. To avoid losing your coins, only use links provided on the official websites for the wallet. Another option is to use an offline hardware wallet.

Hardware-Wallet Theft

Hardware wallets could have built-in-vulnerabilities that create a backdoor for hackers to rob your coins. The scam consists of selling to users a hardware wallet that has been preconfigured with a seed phrase concealed under a scratch card. Unaware of this scam, the user will scratch the card to set up the hardware wallet with that compromised seed. That opens an entry point for hackers to access your wallet and drain your coins. To avoid such scam, only purchase hard wallets from trusted sources.

Phishing

Phishing e-mails are frequently sent by scammers in an attempt to steal information from bitcoin owners. One example was the Bitfinex phishing attempt. Phishing e-mail may request information, such as your crypto wallets or your username and password. Bitcoin and altcoin owners can be tricked by phishing websites to upload their crypto wallets, provide private keys, or release sign-in information. Never comply with such requests.

Hacking Payment Gateway

Investors should be aware that they could lose their coin despite using the correct address and the proper online exchange payment gateway. Hackers have developed payment gateways that look legit. These hackers use these payment gateways to trick online exchanges to validate transfer to hackers' accounts. Hackers thus trick the hosting online exchange to direct a transaction to a fake account.

Initial Coin Offering (ICO) Fraud

An ICO is a method used to raise capital for an existing or a newly created cryptocurrency. Because ICOs are unregulated, it exposes the investor to significant scamming risks. These risks could be the results of scammers creating a fake ICO to rob investors' money or criminals impersonating a legitimate ICO and tricking investors into paying them instead of the real company. To avoid ICO fraud, investors must conduct enough research on an ICO before purchasing it. They should also verify the legitimacy of the ICO by checking on websites such as CoinDesk.

E-mail Scams

Scammers are increasingly using e-mails to lure investors to log into their account. Recently some holders of cryptocurrency accounts were sent deceitful e-mails from a bogus address pertaining to be MyEtherWallet. The e-mail requested users to log into a provided fake version of MyEtherWallet for the purpose of securing their coins. People who logged in to that provided site unwillingly provided the scammer with pertinent account information and exposed their MyEtherWallet to being drained off coins. E-mail scammers frequently act as wallet providers and generally look for susceptible individuals whom they persuade to give out their private key. As a rule, never provide your private key to anyone.

Chapter 9

How to Minimize the Hacking of Your Coins

Many investors enter the world of cryptocurrencies unaware of the security breaches. Investors should never totally trust an online exchange security system. Protect your account by adding multiple security precautions. Below are some of the best ways to shield your cryptocurrency from hackers.

Private Key

Always confirm that the web wallet's address you are using is the correct one. Never open a link from an unknown source or send your coins to a doubtful web wallet or Internet bank.

Antivirus Protection

Install first-class antivirus protection to protect all devices from which you access your account, crypto wallets, or crypto exchanges.

Verify Your Transactions

Check your transaction for the following:

- **The correct amount:** Be very careful of decimal points, because there is a chance that the

decimal point may not be in the place you might think.
- **The recipient address:** It should be exactly what you entered. Always check the first, last, and an intermediary character for correctness.
Fees: Make sure you understand how much you are being charged for transaction fees. It is important to understand that every transaction has an associated tax burden.

Wallet-Recovery Mnemonic

Find a mnemonic that would allow you to recover your crypto wallet in the event that you do not remember your password.

Choose Secure Exchanges

Trade across the most popular and legit exchanges. There is a vast plethora of altcoins available to buy and trade. There are also multiple exchanges where numerous coins are traded. The best advice is to begin with one or two coins. As you gain more experience, you can further diversify your portfolio and trade other coins. Trade only with credible exchanges that are registered on the bitcoin.org website. If you have an account with a centralized exchange like Coinbase, Kraken, or Bitfinex, periodically withdraw your tokens and store them in a hardware wallet. Do not leave large amount of coins on these exchanges.

Authenticate and Secure Your Account

Add two-factor authentication to all your crypto accounts. Use a Google two-factor authentication or the two-factor authenticator provided by your online exchange to protect your account. If you have a Coinbase account, setup the Coinbase vault and two-factor authentication for any sends off-site.

Secure E-mail

Before opening an account with any online exchanges, create a specific e-mail to use for that account. Each account should be associated to a different e-mail account.

Secure Password

Set up complex passwords consisting of letters (upper and lower cases), numbers, and special characters. The passwords should be at least eight characters long. The passwords for your e-mail and cryptocurrency account should be different.

Secure Your Cell Phone

Request your cell-phone provider to add a passcode and a *do not port* SIM card feature to your cell-phone account. Avoid sharing your cell phone with anyone.

Use Decentralized Exchanges.

With decentralized exchanges, it is difficult for hackers to have access to your account unless you compromise your login information or disclose your private keys. Decentralized exchanges do not have access to your private keys. Should a decentralized exchange be hacked, it would be very difficult for hackers to steal your private keys.

Chapter 10

Understanding the Risks

Lack of Regulatory Oversight

The nonregulatory nature of cryptocurrencies comes with its pitfalls. The lack of a central authority managing all transactions and the relative anonymity of transactions make investing in cryptocurrency a very risky endeavor. Digital currencies are treacherous instruments that are highly vulnerable to cyber attacks. There is no agency or a reporting system to which you can refer if your account is compromised.

Various government agencies and the court system are scrutinizing cryptocurrencies' activities. Two cease-and-desist letters from the boards of securities in the states of Texas and North Carolina have crippled Bitconnect's operation, leaving investors with massive losses.

ICO is method used to raise fund that lacks transparency and oversight. Some ICOs are launched to fraudulently prey on investors. Be very cautious before investing in any ICO. Research the authenticity and validity of these coins. Because of the increased interest in ICOs and digital currencies, regulatory agencies have become increasingly aggressive in tracking the activities of cryptocurrencies and ICOs.

Uptrends and Downtrends

Cryptocurrencies are predominantly characterized by the high fluctuation in their price. These price vacillations have enabled speculators to reap significant profits while deterring others from entering into any crypto investment. It is projected that in a few years, the price of bitcoin will exponentially rise. The reality remains unclear. Given the current trend, there is a high suspicion that the price will continuously rise. Investors who choose to hold their bitcoin on a long-term basis could reap greater profits. However, investors should understand that bitcoin goes through many price corrections that could significantly drop its value. Bitcoin price fluctuations are driven by many factors, some of which are presented below.

Bad Press versus Good Press

Any information that supports or hinders the acceptance of bitcoin leads to a flux in its price. Such information could be geopolitical events, government regulations, bitcoin-exchange hacking, or headline news about bitcoin. Many cryptocurrencies, including bitcoin and bitconnect, have been victim of bad press, resulting in a drastic drop in their value.

Security Breaches

When security vulnerabilities are exposed, the public reacts with skepticism about the viability of bitcoin. Despite several exchange scams and hacks, pundits of cryptocurrencies remain overall optimistic that virtual currencies will revolutionize the current financial system. There have been numerous reported breaches, a reminder that cryptocurrency is still a highly vulnerable asset. Despite the security provided by the blockchain technology, security breaches are still prevalent. Hackers continuously look for loopholes to steal your cryptocurrency.

Regulation and Taxes

The IRS treats cryptocurrencies as personal property. Therefore, buying and selling cryptocurrencies is similar to buying and selling gold or stock. The new tax law considers trading a digital currency for another one a taxable event. The law bars cryptocurrency owners from deferring capital gains taxes when trading one type of virtual currency for another one.

The decision to consider bitcoin as a form of property for tax purposes could suggest stronger regulations to come. Harsh regulation could hinder the adoption of bitcoin and consequently slow its global acceptance, which is critical for its overall utility in society.

Considering bitcoin an asset rather that a currency adds complexity for users who want to use it as a method of payment or trade it for other cryptocurrencies. On the other hand, recognizing bitcoin as an asset reinforces its acceptance by federal authorities.

Stop-Loss Order[31]

Another risk that could drive cryptocurrencies' prices down is a stop-loss-exacerbated profit taking. A stop-loss order limits a loss on a coin or locks in a profit. Stop-loss orders are generally set at 10 percent or 20 percent lower than the virtual coin's price. Using a stop-loss order to lock in profit could drive prices down; creating a rapid cascade that further adversely affects the price of the coin. Such a downward trend is sometimes amplified by investors' fears about losing their principal.

Chapter 11

Legality of Cryptocurrency

The legal status of bitcoin and other altcoins differs significantly from country to country and is still subject to change. While some governments consider their use illegal, many others have granted cryptocurrencies a status of commodity or currency. As cryptocurrencies gain in popularity, tax authorities, law-enforcement agencies, and regulators are defying one of the core concepts of digital assets known as decentralization by enforcing regulations to control it.

Internal Revenue Services

According to the IRS, cryptocurrencies are considered properties. The tax implication imposes investors to track gains or losses on all cryptocurrencies transactions and report them to the IRS. The required record-keeping creates a compliance headache unless online marketplaces create a ledger of investors' transactions.

Federal Election Commission

The decision of the Federal Election Commission to allow political campaigns to accept microdonations of bitcoin validates the acceptance of bitcoin. This ruling provides more incentive to lawmakers to accept rather than reject bitcoin and other cryptocurrencies. As many regulatory groups embrace and validate the use of bitcoin, the fledgling industry of virtual currency will continue to grow. However, using bitcoin for campaign financing could have the adverse effect of encouraging individuals to illegally hide their political donations of bitcoin.

Legislative Authority

The power vested in Congress to regulate commerce with foreign countries and among US states and to regulate the value of coins poses a threat to the acceptance of virtual currency. This chamber can exercise that power to ban cryptocurrencies if these coins pose a risk to the financial stability of the United States. Courts can also prohibit or limit the scope of virtual currencies by basing their ruling on existing regulations or statutes.

Illegal Activities

Cryptocurrencies can be used for illegal activities, such as money laundering, financing crime, and terrorism sponsoring. That poses a threat to governmental institutions and could lead to stronger regulations. In

2013, the Financial Crimes Enforcement Network released a statement requiring exchanges and administrators of virtual currencies to register as money-services businesses. The purpose of that requirement was to prevent financial exchanges from being used for illegal activities.

Money Laundering

Money laundering is very prevalent in the world of cryptocurrency. The inherent nature of crypto blockchain allows for transfers worldwide, making it easy to use virtual currencies for money laundering. Despite the best regulations put in place by various governments, it will be difficult to eliminate these illegal transactions. Some cryptocurrencies provide an easy avenue for money laundering. This is the case for darkcoin, which combines transactions to increase the complexity of tracking its trades.

Monetary Policy

The Federal Reserve's current monetary policies are subject to changes, especially with the constantly growing size of the crypto market. If the Federal Reserve wanted to change its policy regarding virtual currency, the impact on the global market would be insignificant.

Market Environment

Many predict that cryptocurrencies will continue to gain popularity and that the need to accept these currencies will continue to grow. Many online marketplaces provide the ability to exchange bitcoin into fiat currency. Moreover, many merchants are gradually accepting bitcoin as a method of payment.

Taxable Cryptocurrencies Events

Some of the crypto transactions with tax implications include:

- Mining coins: Mining generates new coins that are treated as ordinary income at the fair market value of the coin on the day it was mined.
- Trading cryptocurrencies: This activity produces capital gains or losses.
- Spending cryptocurrency: The IRS tax code views spending your coin as a tax event that may generate capital gain or loss.
- Exchanging one coin for another: Using a cryptocurrency to purchase another one is a taxable event considered as capital gain or loss.
- Receiving payments in cryptocurrency: Any exchange of cryptocurrency for a service, salary,

or product is considered ordinary income at the market value of the coin.
- Converting cryptocurrency to fiat money: This conversion is treated as selling your coin and is treated as a capital gain or loss.
- Air drops:[32] They are viewed as ordinary income on the day of the offering. If transacted, they are categorized as capital gain.
- ICO: ICO generates new capital and is considered ordinary income.

[1] **Volatility:** Rate or degree of fluctuation of the value of an asset. A high volatility is associated with rapid fluctuations in price and generally implies a risker investment.

[2] **Digital asset:** Intangible good with an intrinsic or acquired value, which can be owned or controlled to produce value. Within the context of cryptocurrency, digital assets possess an economic or financial value.

[3] **Bitcoin:** Digital currency created for use in peer-to-peer online transactions. Bitcoin is an example of a digital asset that falls under the category of cryptocurrency.

[4] **Cryptocurrency:** Digital currency that uses cryptography to secure its transactions, control the production of more units, and confirm its transfer.

[5] **Digital currency:** Intangible payment method available in an electronic form. Its electronic nature allows for easy transfer of ownership and instantaneous transactions. Synonyms of digital currency include digital money, electronic money, or electronic currency.

[6] **Altcoin:** Alternative to bitcoin. This describes any cryptocurrency that is not a bitcoin. Examples of altcoins include litecoin, ethereum, ripple, and

monero, to name a few.

[7] **Cryptography:** Process of storing and transmitting coded data using encryption to protect its integrity and secrecy.

[8] **Decentralization:** Process of allocating and dispersing roles, functions, authority, resources away from a central location or authority. Decentralization provides direct exchange or communication among users (peer to peer) through an automated process.

[9] **Confirmation:** Validation that a transaction was processed by bitcoin miners and added to a new block on the blockchain.

[10] **Peer-to-peer network:** Computer application architecture configured to partition tasks or workloads with everyone or with selected users. Allows file sharing and grants participants equal privileges and equipotent participation.

[11] **Blockchain:** Digital, decentralized, public ledger that records and stores chronologically and publicly all transactions made in bitcoin or any other cryptocurrency.

[12] **Satoshi:** Alias for the inventor of bitcoin. Satoshi is used to represent the smallest measurement of bitcoin: 1 Satoshi = 0.00000001 BTC. An illustration would be to compare a Satoshi to a penny.

[13] **Double spend:** Process by which the same single digital currency is reused for another transaction.

[14] **Open-source code:** Computer program for which the copyright holder grants access to his or her coding information to allow anyone to inspect, modify, or enhance it.

[15] **Fungibility:** Ability of a good or a commodity to be replaced or exchanged by another one of equal part or quantity.

[16] **Mining:** Peer-to-peer mathematical calculations of the bitcoin and altcoin networks used to secure and verify bitcoin transactions. It is the process by which transactions are verified and added to the public ledger, known as the blockchain. It is one means through which new bitcoin are released.

[17] **BTC:** Bitcoin

[18] **Private key:** Secret piece of data stored in a wallet that allows the transaction of bitcoins. Anyone with access to your private keys can spend your bitcoin.

[19] **Coin:** Used to refer to cryptocurrency (bitcoin and altcoins).

[20] **Encryption:** Method of encoding information or data by converting it into a code to secure and prevent unauthorized access.

[21] **Two-factor authentication:** Method of confirming a user's claimed identity by requiring not only a password and username but also a critical piece of information that only the user should know or have.

[22] **Retracement:** Temporary price reversal of a coin during a prevailing trend.

[23] **Candlestick:** Display of the lowest, highest, opening, and closing prices of a coin during a set timeframe. It is called candlestick because of its shape resembling a candle.

[24] **Bollinger squeeze:** Area of the Bollinger bands that show a narrowing of the bands. The two bands move closer to each other. It indicates a decrease in volatility.

[25] **White paper:** A document released by a developer of coin to explain to the investors the objective of the coin, its innovation, limitations, and future plans.

[26] **Valuation:** Also called market capitalization, it represents the total market value of a specific cryptocurrency. Mathematically it is the number of outstanding coins multiplied by the price of the coin.

[27] **Fiat money:** This term is used to describe an official currency used in a country. In the United States, fiat money is the US dollar.

[28] **Hype:** Exaggerated price projection that is not based

in truth or in fact

[29] **Buy the rumor and sell the news:** Trading practice consisting in buying based on the belief in a rumor of a given economic report, news, or event and selling once the event passes or the report is released.

[30] **Virtual Private Network:** Technology employing encrypted connection to provide a secure access to a less secure network, such as the Internet

[31] **Stop-loss order:** Order to buy or sell a cryptocurrency when it reaches a set price.

[32] **Air drop:** Free coins received from any third party. Air drops include coin freely offered during ICOs, freebies offered as gifts, and free coins delivered to the cryptocurrency to mane a few.

www.ingramcontent.com/pod-product-compliance
Lightning Source LLC
Chambersburg PA
CBHW031546210526
45464CB00003B/1171